The Call Center Chronicles:
Cubicle Controversies

B. Louise LoCastro

ISBN-13: 978-1534869370

ISBN-10: 1534869379

DEDICATION

I would like to dedicate this book to anyone who has survived it, is currently suffering through it, or is about to endure it. It is a tough work world out there. If you are not a doctor, layer, or a politician, you will have to go through one (if not more) "work wars". This is my way of honoring those who work harder than most, but get treated with the least compassion and/or respect. Hats off to you!!

CONTENTS

	Acknowledgments	i
	Introduction	1
1	Assuming My Position	4
2	The Period Predicament	12
3	Uncharitable Givings	14
4	Rotten to the Core	22
5	Earthquakes and Ice Storms, OH MY!	26
6	Half-Naked Truths	31
7	Email Entertainment	36
8	Courage Over Corruption	44

ACKNOWLEDGMENTS

I wanted to send an extra special THANK YOU out to my mother, D. L. LoCastro. It takes one hell of a strong woman to raise a strong-willed woman. You are the epitome of strength, beauty, and grace. All I could ever hope to be is half as inspirational to one person as you have been to me. You are not just my mother, you are my angel on Earth, role model, and very first best friend. Thank you for your continuous love and support. Then, now, and always… I love you for always… and forever!!

INTRODUCTION

If you're reading this I've either resigned, got "terminated"… or I'm going to be. I've worked for this company long enough to know how things go. As long as you go along with whatever, simply smiling and nodding in an agreeable manner, you are safe. Being a "yes" person will get you a long way. However, if you have a fully functioning moral compass, you may find yourself in deep water. Trust and believe me when I say that being a blue-collared girl in a white-collared world is tough. As the slightly younger generation would say about holding your tongue when smart people act dumb… "the struggle is real".

I graduated high-school in nineteen ninety nine. I remember walking out of the front door, on the last day of class, and thinking to myself how amazing it felt to not have to deal with social cliques, bullying, pettiness, and juvenile antics any longer. I was about to venture out into the adult world where there were going to be real responsibilities, consequences, and accountability. Since we were all adults now, everyone has no choice but to follow the rules therefore there would be no more popularity contests. No more favoritism. No more social politics. As long as you work hard and did the right thing, outcomes will consistently sway in your favor. Everything will be fair. I know, I know. "Oh, you poor, sweet, hopeful, and naïve child", I say to myself now.

Once I graduated high-school, I moved forward with my education, and graduated in two-thousand-one with a Bachelor of Arts degree in Educational Psychology with a minor in Human Services. Not realizing until post-graduation that you need a Master's degree in Psychology to actually make money off of your education, I found myself working customer service and executive administrative assistant positions. I worked for a big-named company in the automobile industry as a "call(center) girl" until management changed, and the new guy and I bumped heads, so I had to go. After that, I worked for a commercial construction company as an administrative assistant until they lost a contract and had layoffs. A few months later, I started working for this company. Currently, as I'm writing this, I have been there for almost seven years. Though I have worked my way through my department, and am currently a trainer, to say the road has been rough would be an understatement. It has been one HELL of a journey... if you know what I mean.

What you are about to read is proof that everything I thought about adulthood in the workplace can make you see high school for what it really is; workforce preparation. Though the company name has not been provided and associate's names have been changed to protect the guilty, all of the contents within the following pages are one hundred percent true. Sad, but absolutely true. As sure as I am about the first statement I made at the beginning of this introduction, I am sure that some of you reading this will know exactly what it feels like to go through un-necessary bullshit in the workplace just to pay your necessary bills. I am writing this book in honor, and out of respect, for you all. Someone needs to talk about these things so that others can know they are not alone. I have no problem taking one for the team; I have done it before. You're welcome.

Now... enjoy.

CHAPTER ONE
"ASSUMING MY POSITION"

It's only fair. In order to understand where I am and why I'm here, you have to understand the process that got me to this point. There has definitely been a method to this 'madness'. So, if you're ready, here it goes.

After being laid off for a couple of months from the commercial construction company, and dealing with unemployment's dysfunctional processes, I was doing just about anything I could to find any job. This included, but wasn't limited to, going to career fairs.

One of the career fairs I attended had a representative for the company I am currently working for. To be completely honest, the interview process wasn't much of a 'process'. At the fair, all they had me do was fill out an application and ask if I graduated high school, which I did, so they invited me to the office for a face-to-face interview. During that interview, I was literally asked two questions. The first question was, "Do you have any administrative assistance experience?" And, the second question was, "Do you have any questions for me?" Seriously, that was the two questions. I must have made an impression with my responses as I was called before I made it back home, by the hiring manager, asking if I could start in three weeks. I mean, of course! This girl has bills to pay. I had no clue what I was about to get myself into. None the less, I went.

I remember clearly, sitting in orientation and training, thinking to myself that there is no way in hell I am going to last here after training, so I should probably enjoy and appreciate getting paid for training. It wasn't until I got there, that I realized this company felt an awful lot like a call center. Which, after being laid off for several months, scared the hell out of me. I was afraid that I just unknowingly signed myself up for career suicide.

The new hire training process, though informational, was painful. Myself, along with fourteen other new hires brought onboard from the career fair, sat in a conference room for two weeks reading through two two-inch binders full of repetitive verbiage on processes and programs never heard of before. No power-points. No audio examples. Nothing. Just text. Much to my surprise though, I am (at this moment) still employed with this company. Almost seven years later, I'm still here. 'Why write this book now, then?' Because, to be very honest and direct, I'm pissed off to the highest level of pissedivity. (Yes, that is a B. Louise-ism. You are free to use it however to deem fit.) You would be too, if you were me.

I have genuinely cared about the company, the associates, and both of their development and growth. Since I have been a member of the company, I have seen it through some of the best of times and some of its toughest times, which include multiple layoffs. However, I have reached a point of frustration and concern for my professional growth within the company as I have been over-utilized, unappreciated, and unable to move forward with building my career there.

My current position at the company is Quality Assurance Coordinator, which I have been in "officially" for over three years. I say "officially" as I did not receive that title until the hiring manager, and all of the others assisting with conducting my interview, had been personally trained by me when they were hired... including the Director. During the time that I have been in my current position, the company went through the re-branding process. After the re-branding process was completed, the company created newly titled positions within their the department I evolved from. Some positions were given titles that did not have titles previously and were suddenly considered promotable positions. Unfortunately, as I held some positions before they were actually considered titled and promotable positions, I find myself already behind a certain pay rate then I should be for where I am, based on my professional history and experience with the company as well as the department.

Over the past few years, I have not only conducted trainings, mentoring, coaching, and quarterly quality assessments for multiple positions within the department I initially started in, and at one point of time for multiple office locations, I have also done multiple training sessions for the field staff, call center staff (cross-training initiative), and trained trainers and managers from other departments on our systems and processes to assist with future cross-training department-integration efforts.

For the past over six months, and I have been here for seven years, I have encountered some of the most interesting back-lash for actually doing my job. You see, there are two sides of my job. The one side, which is clearly my favorite, is the part in which I have the opportunity to engage with, coach, and professionally develop the associates. When I am doing those things, I feel as if I am a part of something grander than myself; I am being a part of someone else's personal and professional growth. It is kind of amazing. And, then... there is the other part.

The second part of what I have to do, is the least favored by the associates and (let's be honest) their management teams. Though I am responsible for identifying the categories in which each associate does excel, I also have a responsibility to identify and report on 'opportunities for improvement'. How are these things identified? Both points are based on reports pulled by the quality control team's scoring process which was approved by and signed by the senior management teams. Unfortunately, when most of the associates are hired in as referrals of family and friends of those who already work there (including those connected to people within senior management positions), doing that portion of the job becomes more about feelings than it does about facts. The worst part? Those in management know this, but say nothing, because they are the biggest part of the problem.

Due to those factors, and because I would not let up on reporting those connected associates for their continual lack of quality performance, I found myself under constant attack. At one point, after completing a new hire training, I was pulled aside by my direct supervisor at that time, and was advised that one of the directors had voiced some concerns about me. (Please note, there was only one director.) Those concerns were as follows:

1. You (meaning me) are not training the right material.
2. You (meaning me) are unapproachable.
3. You (meaning me) are coming to work every day looking disheveled, and they are concerned with your health.

You already know I responded! These were my responses.

1. I am training the same exact material that the other trainers in all locations are training from, as the material was created and distributed by a third-party company that our company paid to create it. If that is the case, then all the damn trainers should be in this meeting as well as those who created the material.

2. This came from the same person who complained a week prior that I was engaging too much with her associates and that she would prefer I limit my communication with her staff unless it is training-specific conversation because she wanted them to ask their supervisors more question and not ask me. She needs to pick a damn complaint and stick to it.

3. I have dressed the same way for the past seven years, with dress pants and a blouse, why is this a problem now? And, did someone reference her wearing six-inch heels from the day prior? Yeah, probably not.

4. (Because I added an unnecessary answer, as usual.) Once she comes up with some valid concerns, please let me know, because I have too many things to do than sit here and address issues she is creating because her school buddy (the office manager) is upset because her friends

and family are doing a poor job in quality.

As you have probably already guessed, that only made things worse. What else can I say? Sometimes the truth hurts.

Not too long after that, it was decided that to "safeguard me from the noise" and retaliation from one department for doing my job, they would move me under a different on-location supervisor. The initial point was to move me into a position where I would be the cross-training specialist, between two different departments, to go where I was needed and when I was needed for training, coaching, mentoring, and quality audits. Unfortunately, the harassment continued so they decided to move me solely under the alternative department. Is that where all the issues stopped? I wish.

Upon my transfer over to the alternative department, I was given additional responsibilities, but never an increase to my salary or a change in my title. Regardless of the fact that I could prove, and still can, that they gave me double duties, they never (even to this day) changed my information in the company's systems. Though they gave continual excuses as to why it hadn't been changed over a several month period, I believe we ALL know why they never did so. If they had changed that information within the system, they would have had some explaining to do. Number one, they would've had to explain officially why I was transferred without it being in writing and having my signed consent. And, number two, why I was given additional responsibilities and added to a team that was making more than double my salary, but could not provide me additional compensation or a change in title. I know that they know... that I know. And, nope... still not the end.

For the first time in my seven year tenure with the company, and due to recent layoffs, I was not given a cost of living raise either. To be honest, had *no-one* received one because groups of people were just let go, it wouldn't have bothered me as bad. However, since I was informed that some of the friends and family members of the management team did in fact receive raises... and/or bonuses... I was livid. And, yes... I am speaking about those who fell below in quality standards set in place by corporate's contracted guidelines. Some of them had even fallen below the standard for FOUR consecutive quarters. That is the full year. All of it. But, no... let's reward those who helped contribute to the reason for the layoff and not to those who tried to stop it. (*shaking my head*)

Though that is STILL not the end of my story, I feel like you have a good understanding as to why I am where I am mentally as I am writing this book. Now that you have read about the beginning of my story, and the beginning of the end, it's times to read about the in-betweens...

CHAPTER TWO
"THE PERIOD PREDICAMENT"

I have heard of time management, project management, and employee management, but I have never heard of vagina management! I bet you want clarification on that one. Well, that's what I am here for.

Occasionally, all associates of the company receive emails from the Administrative Assistants of the executive management team, regarding updates to policies and procedures. These emails go out to all associates, regardless of location, position, or gender. This happens regardless of the policy's content. Below you will see a copy of the email that was distributed regarding feminine hygiene. You're going to absolutely love this, I promise.

Good morning,

For our ladies' convenience, extra sanitary napkins and tampons will be held by the receptionist at each of our office locations.

Should you need a product please see the receptionist at your location to sign for the product you are requesting. You will have 30 days to replenish what you use. If you do not replenish that supply within 30 days, you will receive a reminder. Not replenishing that product prior to 60 days may result in a written warning by your direct supervisor.

(Provided all location's contact persons' names and extension numbers.)

Thanks,
(Executive Administrative Assistant)

So, yeah. What they are pretty much saying is that you can come on up and grab an emergency maxi pad or tampon, but you better put one back within sixty days or your ass is grass. Seriously, folks? If that is the biggest issue your company has, you are doing pretty good. I don't know, though. Maybe if you spent as much time worrying about your associates and management successfully completely tasks up to quality standards, as you were about regulating tampon usage and outlining disciplinary actions for their use, then the company would not have deal with layoffs at least four times in seven years. Just a thought.

CHAPTER THREE
"UNCHARITABLE GIVINGS"

Of all the things I have almost been fired for, I think informing my co-workers, management, and Human Resources of a fundraiser being hosted to benefit a former colleague who was battling cancer has to be my favorite. Yes, you read that right. As it turns out, unless the company receives a tax write off for 'charitable-givings', they couldn't care less about their employees... or, let's be honest, charity.

In order for you to grasp and appreciate how epically insensitive and morally bankrupt this company is, I have to back the story up a little bit. A background story, if I may.

Shortly after I started working for the company, I started making friends pretty quickly. One of the first people I befriended worked for the facilities department, "Denise". Let me be direct, I know we all need jobs because we all have bills to pay. However, Denise took a lot more crap from the company than I would have.

Denise was given the title "Facilities Specialist", which was honestly a fancy way of saying 'receptionist' and 'handy-woman'. Not only was she responsible for answering doors and phones, managing sign-in sheets, taking shipping orders, updating and maintaining seating charts, making lunch orders, processing terminations, creating meeting packets, and managing schedules for senior management and Human Resources, but they also tasked her multiple times to repair holes in the carpet, climb into the ceiling to try to locate leaks, haul dozens of crates (during a few of the company lay-offs), and moving around company equipment to prepare for hosted events. And, yes... on her own. Do you know, Human Resources even made her the Captain of the "Emergency Preparedness Committee", and advised her that, should there be a fire in the building, she was required to stay inside until she could confirm that all other associates had vacated? My response? "Oh, HELL to the NO!!" I told Denise that if she sees me running, she should run too, because I don't run. I said, and I quote, "If an alarm sounds, you grab your purse and keys... and then you leave! They can replace this broken down building, but they can't replace YOU. I will carry your ass out of here, kicking and screaming, if I have to. I am not afraid of you or them... GOT IT?!" My question is, why wouldn't any of those individuals providing those directives volunteer their damn selves to be the 'last one out'? That's right; they're punks. None the less, I digress.

After almost six years with the company, Denise handed in her two week notice. Due to her being the only member of her household generating income due to her mother's health conditions, they decided to move out of state to be closer to family that could offer the kind of assistance they so badly needed.

Prior to Denise's departure, Human Resources did decide to throw her 'farewell' bash. Two weeks prior to leaving the company, Human Resources sent out this email.

Good afternoon,

As most of you may know by now, Denise, is moving on from the company and her last day is May 9. If you don't know her, she's our Receptionist at the front desk. Denise has been with us for 6 years and has become a staple here at (location of the office).

To show our appreciation for all the hard work she does around here we will secretly accept contributions for her move out of state. If you would like to make a contribution, you may do so up until May 8th. See the attached flyer for further details.

We will also have light refreshments to celebrate her last day, May 9, between 1:00 p.m. – 2:00 p.m. We will meet in Executive Conference Room #2 by the elevators.

Most importantly ...DON'T TELL DENISE! We want this to be a surprise!

Thanks,
(Executive Administrative Assistant)

And, this is what they flyer said...

Denise will be moving out of state. In an effort to show our appreciation and assist her with her move we are secretly holding a collection. This can help with gas, new household items, etc. If interested, please turn in your contribution to (Human Resource Contacts) by May 8th.

Please join us for light refreshments on Friday, May 9th from 1:00 - 2:00 in Executive Conference Room 2 to personally give Denise your well wishes.

Most importantly...DON'T TELL DENISE! We want this to be a surprise!

Needless to say, her farewell send-off went off without a hitch. Denise was so humbled by the words and kindness her colleagues showed her. She had even mentioned to me, as I helped her carry out her flowers, balloons, and gifts, how she wished she didn't have to move because, the friends she had made during her employment with the company, have become more like her honorary family at heart. I just whole-heartedly wish this was the saddest part of this chapter. Unfortunately, it isn't.

Denise left the company two weeks, to the day, that her and her mother were scheduled to move out of state. Two *days* before they were scheduled to move, Denise received a phone call from one of her doctor's that would change the course of the next several months of her and her mother's life. Denise received word that the final physical and tests she had done revealed that she did, in fact, have ovarian cancer. If God gives his toughest battles to His strongest soldiers, Denise had to be Corporal.

Though Denise is one of the strongest people I know, between the stress of the move, her mother's health, bills piling up, and now her health concerns, it all had become too much for her to carry on her own. She really needed help and support.

Following a conversation I had with Denise, we came up with an idea. A few days later, I sent out the following email out to all those associates who worked closely with Denise for the past six years, including HR.

Good morning;

As some of you may already know one of my very best friends, Denise ("Facilities Specialist" for the company from June 2008 – May 2014), was set to relocate with her mother this past Memorial Day weekend to be closer to her family as her mother has been ill for quite a while. Denise gave her two-week's notice at work, and packed hers and her mother's belongings, only to find out two days before moving that she (herself) was diagnosed with Ovarian Cancer. Right now, she could really use some support.

She is still supposed to go for more scans, surgery, and treatment. However, since her insurance ran out, her specialists all want to be paid up front before they will touch her. She has applied for medical assistance through the state, but was told that she is still being evaluated and it can take up to 30 days before she hears anything back regarding a status of her request for assistance. Though she has stressed the importance of the situation, they didn't seem to care. She told her doctor what is going on and they have to put her surgery on hold, and advised her to talk to the finance/billing department.

Yes, she left her job... but it was to start a new life and so that her mother could enjoy what is left of hers (as her mother also has cancer). Though all her and her mother have asked for is prayers... I know they could use this support.

Due to the circumstances, I have started a fundraiser to assist with the medical bills, surgery, and treatment Denise will need to battle this disease. Though she is my best friend, there is only so much I can do by myself.

The link below will take you to the fundraiser site for the "Denise's Cancer Support Fund". If you are unable to help, I completely understand, but maybe you could pass the word along to those who might.

(Provided link.)

Thank you, in advance, for any form of support you can provide for Denise during her fight.

Best Regards, B. Louise LoCastro

Good deed, right? Well, I thought so too. Unfortunately, we are the only ones who share that view as I found myself sitting in the office of the Senior Director with Human Resources two hours later. As it turns out, 'charitable giving' only pertains to company-based initiatives that conclude with organizational recognition and tax write-offs. The Senior Director and Human Resource Business Partner informed me that, though I was not breaking any Codes of Compliance as they stood, that I was facing termination due to the release of a previous employee's personal information... even though it was public knowledge and was permitted by Denise. I guess it is a double standard. I mean, technically, they divulged her personal information without her consent to offer some assistance with her relocation as they knew that she had no way of doing it on her own. And, you can guess that they didn't like the fact that I brought that up... at all.

Prior to leaving the office, I was told that they had to think about how they were going to handle 'this situation' and would let me know what their decision was as soon as they made one. I remember leaving that office thinking that if they did decide to fire me, I was going to contact every single damn news outlet I could across the country letting them know how non-compassionate, morally incompetent, and self-serving the company was. I was not playing games. I genuinely felt a sense of rage I had never felt before. Truth be told, I think they knew it because it took them two weeks to decide how they were going to handle 'the situation'.

I was placed on a 'Level II' disciplinary action for a sixty day period. What does that mean you ask? In a nutshell, I could not apply for a promotable position, for the next couple of months. (*rolling my eyes*) I honestly, to this day, believe that the only reason why I was placed on a disciplinary action at all was because the Senior Director knew that I had a copy of the Compliance policy proving that I had not violated anything, but had already threatened my job, so he couldn't just do nothing and acknowledge that he was wrong. God forbid. It is still a damn joke to me.

From that point moving forward, though I volunteered and supported charitable organizations on my personal time and through book sales, I adamantly refused to participate in any company sponsored charity events. They knew better, too. Every time they walked around collecting donations, they purposely skipped my aisle. I give to purpose and cause, not just when a company is looking for a solid tax write off.

CHAPTER FOUR
"ROTTEN TO THE CORE"

Core values. Every company claims to have them. But, do they really? I have been told multiple times that, though they know how hard I work, that perception is reality and some people perceive me incorrectly based on what they hear from others. Well, I have decided to break down some of the core values, how they could be misperceived by those from the outside, and why I don't necessarily give a damn about what shady and lying-ass people think of me.

Let's start out with 'integrity', shall we? Integrity, simply put, is doing the right thing. For instance, if you know one of your associates are receiving their fourth consecutive below average score (by corporate standards), and they have been coached and retrained multiple times, but see no improvement... you get rid of them. You do not promote them and then complain about the department's QA being "too involved" with the floor staff. That is the QA's job. Where is the integrity in that? Exactly.

Nonexistent. Moving right along.

Now, let's talk about 'respect'. Not just respect for others, but also self-respect. Respect for others would mean that you acknowledge when others work hard by rewarding them appropriately. Not just rewarding those within your bloodline, or your best friend's blood line. Respect is *not* about allowing one of your criminal-record-holding managers to terminate a six-year tenured associate for being one minute late because the systems (all of them) are slow as hell, yet allowing that same office manager to knowingly fabricate statements for employees who do their hair or pay them to do their taxes to other managers in other locations in an effort to get them promoted.

Okay, so... 'passion'. Now, I'm not speaking about the tie-me-down, pull-my-hair, and spank me kind that some of you martially connected managers may share. I am speaking to the kind of passion that some of your over-looked tenured associates have towards their quality and completion of their work. You know, the kind of passion that makes some of your associates, such as myself, go above and beyond not just in their contracted roles, but also assist others on a daily basis because that in within their character and general nature. Those are the associates you should be investing in; not those who spend most of their time avoiding their assigned responsibilities and making excuses as to why they cannot met quality standards when others can.

'Excellence'. Now, we already know where I am going with this one. In order to be considered "excellent" at something, especially in business, you must "excel" in multiple arenas. You must have excellent product delivery (not fall short on following through with your contractual agreements with your clients), have all your associates at least meeting the minimal quality standards set in place by the corporate guidelines (not having at least ninety-plus percent of one of your office locations falling on an average of ten to twenty percent below the minimum requirement for at least the fourth consecutive quarters), and base your hiring and promoting of associates based qualifications and a proven track record... not favoritism.

"Service", as defined by Merriam-Webster's dictionary, states as follows:

service

noun | ser·vice | \ sər·vəs\

Definition of SERVICE

1   **a :** the occupation or function of serving <in active *service*>
    b : employment as a servant <entered his *service*>

Did you read that? "The occupation or function of servicing"... AND... "employment as a *servant*". (*blank stare*) This is what Servant Leadership is _supposed_ to be about.

You are *supposed* to serve your clients factual information on how you function, as well as your company's *realistic* capabilities. You are not supposed to provide your clients with misleading information so they then have unrealistic expectations of what can be completed based on the current functionality of resources (or lack thereof) and the amount of associates employed. You are *supposed* to have people in leadership roles who utilize their knowledge and expertise to assist with the development and growth of their associates, the department, and the company, *not* bosses who abuse the power of their position.

Again, core values mean nothing if they are not valued. You can say and post all the verbiage you want to but, if there are no actions taking place to enforce those values, they become irrelevant and even, in some cases, contradictory. It is just not a good look or, as one of the management team's favorite term goes, perception.

CHAPTER FIVE
"EARTHQUAKES AND ICE STORMS, OH MY!"

Whatever shakes, rattles, or rolls better not do so on company time. If it does, you are kind of screwed. Who cares if the earth actually *does* move under your feet? You have calls to make, productivity to exceed, and a corporate office that sees you as only a number to make numbers.

I live and work in what is known as the 'DMV' area; more specifically, the District of Columbia, Maryland, and Virginia tristate region. In August 2011, I decided to take my first entire week off since I had started with the company two years prior. Unfortunately, on Tuesday, August 23 at approximately 1:50 PM, as I was at the salon with my head foiled-up with bleach, Virginia experienced its first 5.8 earthquake. The tremors from the earthquake extended for miles. Honestly, I think that was the most scared I have ever been. I am from this area so unlike Californians, who experience earthquakes on a semi-regular basis, I thought I was experiencing 'the end of days'. I know, I am definitely a sissy when it comes to things like that. I do not play with mother nature. She is a beast.

Not only did we have that earthquake but, later on that week, the back-currents of Hurricane Irene swept through the northeast region, and essentially flooded out the basement apartment (which, for those who know me could confirm that I reference frequently as "the hole of Hell") I was living in with my now *ex-husband*. (That is a whole other book!) That week I learned to not only pick better weeks in which to vacation, I also learned upon my return to work, the true value the company placed on its associates and the associates (and their families') quality of life.

Upon my return to the office, like I do as soon as I come in every day, I checked my email. The following is the email that was sent out to the associates the morning after the earthquake struck.

From: (Human Resources)
Sent: Wednesday, August 24, 2011 9:43 AM
To: All Offices
Subject: Yesterday's Earthquake - Departures

Good morning,

As we are all aware, yesterday afternoon around the two o'clock hour in the afternoon, the State of Virginia experienced an earthquake that registered as a 5.8 on the rector scale. Unfortunately, due to this, it was reported that multiple associates vacated without advising their direct supervisor or waiting on the directive that permission was given to leave for them day.

Though we here at (company name) hold our employee's safety at the top of our list of priorities, we hope that you as associates take into consideration our business needs. Moving forward, we request that you confirm with your direct supervisor that it is permissible to leave for the day, prior to doing so. Not confirming such details may constitute a verbal warning here after.

Again, we value you as employees and appreciate your commitment to providing the best service to our clients regardless of the circumstance.

(Human Resources)

So, what they were pretty much saying is that your safety, your family's safety, and the overall quality of your psyche, is less important to the company than you spending that final three hours calling people and leaving messages because, let's face it, you are replaceable.

Though I would love to say I was surprised, I can't. Between the end of February and the beginning of March in 2010, there were two consecutive snow storms that hit the DMV area. These storms left in their wake over two feet of snow and ice on the ground and road ways. In some areas there was even more. Not only did all the local and county government offices shut down, but the Federal Government also called in a State of Emergency. Under those guidelines, anyone caught attempting to travel on the roads would be ticketed, towed, and fined. Did the company shut down? Hell no. They did, however, post a recording on the 'weather line' stating that if you didn't feel comfortable or safe driving in the current conditions, you needed to hang up, call your supervisor back, and explain why you were not able to make it into the office. Oh yeah, and if you didn't have any of your paid-time-off available, you were not getting paid... and receiving an attendance occurrence, better known as 'unscheduled leave without pay', for being a 'call out'.

What did I do? You already know. I hung up, called back, and left a message on my direct supervisor's voicemail, as I was directed to do so. This is EXACTLY what I said on the voicemail:

> "Good morning, (supervisor's name). It's B. Louise. I'm only leaving this message because I was directed to do so by the Weather Line. Apparently, (the company) does not watch the news. All of the local and county government offices have been shut down, and the Federal Government has also called in a State of Emergency. Under those guidelines, anyone caught attempting to travel on the roads will be ticketed, towed, and fined. Since it is hard enough to get white-out and pens, I doubt the company is willing to reimburse for possible tow fines, medical bills, and/or car damage, so I'll be returning when the State of Emergency is lifted. We'll talk later. Have a good one!"

Was that snarky? Hell yes, it was. And, guess what? I really didn't give a damn. Though they apparently thought they have the power to make decisions like that above the government, they don't. Listen, I work to live... not live to work. Therefore, let's be clear, my health and safety (as well as my family's) will always take precedence over company guidelines. Always.

CHAPTER SIX
"HALF NAKED TRUTHS"

Please don't get me wrong, I am all for company policies. I just believe that, if you are going to implement regulated organizational policies, you should probably make sure that they are legally enforceable and that members of your senior management team do not contradict those policies. And, yes... I have examples.

With social media being one of the top mainstream ways people generally stay connected with friends, family, and close colleagues, the company released a new online social-media based policy. The policy stated if you are caught posting anything negative about the company publicly, you would be terminated immediately. It didn't take too long before a couple of victims fell prey of this trap.

One day, upon my arrival to the office, I realized that there were two empty seats in the row behind me. When I asked the Director of Operations at that time why they were termed, the only response I received was "The Online Posting Policy". So, you guessed it. As soon as I made it back to my desk, I had to check it out. Below you will see what I saw, from one of those associates.

Name Protected
May 31, 2013 ·

TGIF I couldn't take another day in this insane place

Like   Comment   Share

So, naturally, my first generalized question is... what the Hell?! First of all, the company name isn't mentioned in this status update. Secondly, the information written is what most nine-to-fivers think on Fridays. Lastly, how the Hell are you viewing this posting if the privacy settings are listed under 'Friends Only'. This just sets off a whole list of additional questions. Questions such as, "Are there members of the management team on social media just to stalk the employees?" My guess is, yes. However, it would not have been me they fired for this situation. At least not without a fight.

You see, Maryland (the state in which the corporate office is stationed), is considered an "at will" employment state. What does that mean exactly? According to Wikipedia, "At-will employment is a term used in U.S. labor law for contractual relationships in which an employee can be dismissed by an employer for any reason (that is, without having to establish "just cause" for termination), and without warning. When an employee is acknowledged as being hired "at will", courts deny the employee any claim for loss resulting from the dismissal." So, pretty much, you can be wearing the wrong color shoes, or blink too many times in a nanosecond, and get fired. Don't get me wrong, I would have left. I would have also let that specific Director's skeletons out of the closet.

The irony of it all? The Director at that time, who was responsible for the implementation and execution of this new policy, was living a double life. By day, she was the Director of Operations. She was one of the people, alongside just one other Director at that time, responsible for an entire department that spanned out to another state. At night, this Director was working on her acting and modeling career. If you were to go online and Google her name, you would find air-brushed photos of her dressed-up half-naked ass planted all over it. And, yes... I looked it up as soon as I had heard about it, but so did everyone else. Judge away.

I just think that if those associates got termed for postings that were generalized, the Director should have been termed as well. I mean, really?! You want our clients to look up the Director of your Operations department, find those pictures, and then be disappointed when they meet her in person? You are okay with *that* being a representation of the company? Sleazy, fake, and made-up? I'm not saying it is far from the truth. I'm just saying that if you are going to implement policies, they should be all inclusive and make some damn sense.

In an effort to prove my point further, I would like to include a excerpt from the 'Employee Handbook', which clearly explains how they are all subjective and not all inclusive. The following statement comes from the bottom portion of the '"DISCLAIMERS" section.

> *"Employment at (the company) is at-will, which means both the associates and (the company) have the right to terminate employment at any time, with or without notice, and with or without cause. Nothing in the Handbook constitutes a contract, express or implied, or creates a legally obligation on the part of (the company) or any of its associates. In addition, the Handbook does not alter the at-will nature of the employment relationship between (the company) and its associates. (The company) does not offer tenured or guarantee employment and nothing in this Handbook or any other document or statement shall limit the right to terminate employment at-will or limit (the company's) right to transfer, demote, suspend, discipline or change the terms and conditions of employment at its sole discretion."*

Um. What?! So, the company just spent God knows how much money to pay the Legal Counsel to write up a sixty-something page document that serves absolutely no purpose. None. According to this portion of the disclaimer, the handbook, nor the policies written within it, hold any weight and can be altered at any point, without cause or justification, at convenience of the company or its associates based on whomever is looking to benefit at any given time. Now, I only took a few pre-law classes before I choose a psychology major, but I know a useless investment in time and documentation when I see it. I mean, I have to justify why I need the company to purchase twenty binders for a new-hire training class, to train the company's newly hired associates, or even a box of pens, but you can find the funding for this?! Okay.

To be honest, I'm not sure what is worse. The fact that, according to the disclaimer, none of the policies within the handbook are set policies, or the fact that the company spends valuable time and monetary resources issuing these handbooks, making associates complete online compliance modules, and facilitating trainings for policies and procedures that, at the end of the day, have no bearings. None. Again, why? So you can give your clients a false sense of security? Great job. I applaud you.

CHAPTER SEVEN
"EMAIL ENTERTAINMENT"

I can't stand 'email gangsters'. You know what I mean. The type people who act all big and bad because they are sitting behind a computer screen. I never quite understood how some people could become so brave and seem to forget you actually know and interact with them in real life.

Those who know me in real life could confirm that I do not allow anyone to insult my intelligence or attack my character without setting facts straight. Want to think you sit on a pedestal because of your title? No problem. Let me remind you that some people actually don't give a damn about your power complex and have absolutely no qualms with knocking you off your royal stool.

Because I have made a vow to myself, as well as everyone reading this, I have decided to share a couple of emails between myself and members of the management team, so you can get a real-life look into corporate politics and inner-office power-struggles. Yes, I will provide you the with a brief synopsis of what situations or circumstances led up to these correspondences, as well as the conclusion.

Here it goes.

Brief Synopsis: *My mother had to get a double thyroidectomy due to Thyroid Cancer issues, therefore I applied and was approved to receive intermediate FMLA. The following are the correspondence between myself and Human Resources.*

From: *B. Louise LoCastro*
Sent: *Monday, November 04, 2013 8:40 AM*
To: *(Supervisor)*
Cc: *(Human Resources)*
Subject: *FMLA - Week of 10/28/13-11/1/13!*

Good morning!

I just wanted to advise you both that last week, 10/28/13-11/1/13, I was out for FMLA the amount of hours listed below.

10/28/13 – 8 hours (all day)
11/1/13 – 3 hours (clocked in at 11AM)

Best Regards,
B. Louise LoCastro

From: (Human Resources)
Sent: Monday, November 04, 2013 2:18 PM
To: B. Louise LoCastro
Cc: (Supervisor)
Subject: RE: FMLA - Week of 10/28/13-11/1/13!

Hi B. Louise,

Thanks so much for the update. I need to make sure I have my records correct. For the month of October, you used 8 hours of FMLA on 10/17 , 10/28, and 10/30? The total for the month of October is 24 hours? For tracking purposes, please provide me with a weekly account of your FMLA time used. Please do not provide me with future appointments. Please make sure you continue to provide your manager with future scheduled appointments. Thanks again for keeping me updated. Have a great night.

(Human Resources)

Six months later...

From: B. Louise LoCastro
Sent: Monday, April 21, 2014 9:27 AM
To: (Supervisor)
Cc: (Human Resources)
Subject: FMLA week of 4/14-4/19

Good morning, (Human Resources);

This email is to simply inform you that on Wednesday (4/16), I used eight (8) hours for FMLA purposes.

Best Regards,
B. Louise LoCastro

From: (Human Resources)
Sent: Monday, April 21, 2014 10:48 AM
To: B. Louise LoCastro
Cc: : (Supervisor)
Subject: RE: FMLA week of 4/14-4/19

Good Morning B. Louise,
Thanks for the notification.

From: (Human Resources)
Sent: Friday, May 02, 2014 4:18 PM
To: B. Louise LoCastro
Cc: (Supervisor)
Subject: RE: FMLA week of 4/14-4/19

Hi B. Louise,
I hope all is well! Please make sure that you notify me of any FMLA usage within 24 hours of usage. It is important for your FMLA usage to be reported to me timely. Please contact me with any questions or concerns. Thank you.
(Human Resources)

From: B. Louise LoCastro
Sent: Monday, May 05, 2014 7:41 AM
To: (Human Resources)
Cc: (Supervisor)
Subject: RE: FMLA week of 4/14-4/19

Good morning, (Human Resources);

I apologize. Per email communication you sent to me regarding my FMLA time submissions, on 11/5/2013, you stated "For tracking purposes, please **provide me with a weekly account of your FMLA time used**. Please do not provide me with future appointments. Please make sure you continue to provide your manager with future scheduled appointments." This is why I submitted my last usage of time in the manner in which I did. Moving forward I will make sure I provide you with used time within 24 hours. Also, can you please let me know ahead of time if there are changes regarding protocol on the submission of information as soon as those changes are implemented, to ensure that all FMLA matters are taken care of efficiently as possible.

Best Regards,
B. Louise LoCastro

Conclusion: Human Resources got their lives together, and no further communication transpired.

Was I surprised by this situation? No. This came from the same HR representative that could not figure out why she couldn't make color copies from a black and white print out. Yes, this was one of the people responsible for on-boarding new hires and looking out for the company's professional credibility. I know. It's okay to shake your head along with me. Now, on to the next example.

Brief Synopsis #2: I don't kiss my supervisor's ass. I come to work, do my job, do it well, and go home. However, I smoke cigarettes.

From: (Supervisor)
Sent: Tuesday, July 17, 2012 3:11 PM
To: B. Louise LoCastro
Subject: Smoke Breaks

Good Afternoon B. Louise,

I have started noticing a trend of you being away from your desk for extended periods of time throughout the day. While I appreciate that you consistently meet and even exceed your productivity, please keep in mind that any excessive, unauthorized breaks or absence from the employees department during scheduled work hours is against our code of conduct policies. Please be mindful of the amount of time you are spending away from your seat as it is becoming an issue.

One of my concerns with your breaks is that when you are away from your desk, you can frequently be found socializing with Denise in the front entrance area. I know you are interested in advancing with the company and your socializing in the public where people are frequently coming in and out can give people a negative perception about you. Also, this puts Denise in an awkward position, especially as this area is monitored by video cameras.

If you feel as though you need to step away from your desk for more than 5-10 minutes, I encourage you to clock out in order to better handle any personal issues and step away from your desk to utilize the privacy rooms available. Going forward it is imperative that you decrease the amount of breaks taken away from your seat per day.

As a strong entity on the Pre Processing team, I truly value your hard work and dedication to all of your assigned tasks. You are by far a top performer and capable of achieving greatness. I look forward to seeing the greatness you can achieve when maintaining focus on your assigned tasks.

If there is anything I can help you with; questions/concerns, let me know.

Thanks,
(Supervisor)

My Response...

From: B. Louise LoCastro
Sent: Tuesday, July 17, 2012 4:43 PM
To: (Supervisor)
Subject: RE: Smoke Breaks

Good afternoon, (Supervisor);
I hope this email finds you in the best of spirits and health. First and foremost, thank you for acknowledging that I do (in fact) meet (if not exceed) my required productivity each day. And, according to the email you sent to me yesterday, I have had a zero percent quality error rating for the past six months. So, as far as I am concerned... YAY ME!!
Now, about my breaks. You're absolutely right; I take smoke breaks. But, let's be fair. I spend less time on smoke breaks than you take talking about clubbing and "kickin' it" with half the members on this team who are not making productivity and are struggling to measure up to the quality standards, or shopping for shoes online. Are the security cameras catching THAT? Are the other members of the team clocking out when you all are having your little mini-socials, for hours at a time, at your desk? Are you clocking out every time you want to "hit that deal" before it runs out? My guess is no. And, before you try to tell me that you're on your lunch break, or they are on theirs, no one goes on lunch at 9AM every morning and no one is authorized for two two-hour lunch breaks per day. I checked the Code of Conduct Policy just to make sure. Maybe if I was here to make friends instead of a paycheck, you would look overlook my smoke breaks too. I guess you can't win them all. Oh, well.

I would also like to take this opportunity to respond to concerns regarding me spending time speaking with Denise up front in the reception area. You're right, again. I do stand up front and speak with her during my lunch break. She and I would speak at lunch away from the front entrance if she wasn't required to clock-out for lunch

> but stay up front in case deliveries arrive for lunch. Though, I'm pretty sure that is against the law to force someone to work while they are off the clock, it really isn't any of my business and above my pay grade. None the less, moving forward, I will not hang out up front. Hopefully, Denise will actually get a break one day and we can catch up then.
>
> Please let me know if you have any further questions.
>
> Best Regards, B. Louise LoCastro

Conclusion: I totally got written up on a "Level III" for insubordination... but it was totally worth it. Denise finally started getting her lunch breaks, there were no more mini-socials occurring at that supervisors desk for hours on end, and productivity (as well as quality) started to see improvements. So, to the company... you're welcome!!

You see, I am just not a big fan of bullshit. I'm just not. I will absolutely hold myself accountable for whatever it is that I do wrong. Always have. Always will. However, though I am 'slightly unhinged', I am definitely not stupid. So, before you try to throw me under the bus, you might want to make sure I'm not already driving it. Moral of the story? Wash your hands before you start pointing fingers because you never know what *your* fingerprints might leave behind.

CHAPTER EIGHT
"COURAGE OVER CORRUPTION"

One of the values that my mother instilled in me when I was a little girl is to pick your battles but, once you pick them, you need to see them through. She also taught me about courage and standing up for what it right... even if you are standing alone and against all odds. You are never supposed to back down to bullying and you are to live your life in such a way that, at the close of every single day, you can look yourself if the mirror without guilt, regret, or losing any of your self-respect.

Let me be very clear when I say that I don't care what your title and ranking is. I just don't. I believe that you treat a janitor with the same respect you would show towards a CEO. You are supposed to do so because the way you treat others is a direct reflection of your true quality of character.

As I'm sitting here writing this final chapter, you should know that it is such based on the fact that I officially handed in my resignation letter several days ago. No, I did not give them a two-week notice. No, I don't regret it. And, yes... I have never been so sure I wanted to leave a company so badly in my life.

'What in the hell happened?', you may be asking yourself. Well, of course I'm going to tell you! I guess it goes back to that ole-time saying, "Loose Lips Sink Ships".

Two weeks prior to the submittal of my resignation, I came across a phone call in which my full name was mentioned within the first four seconds of the phone call. The call was between an office manager and one of the department supervisors, that just so happen to be husband and wife. I listened to forty seconds of these members of management laugh and discuss how they were not going to allow me the opportunity to get a specific position. There were so many things wrong with that forty second conversation, I am not sure exactly how to prioritize the issues, so I've decided to list them below.

1. I had not even applied for the position.
2. I trained the wife how to preform her associates' core tasks so that she could properly support, manage, and audit her team.
3. I conducted the husband's new hire training.
4. They were talking about how, because I haven't been a floor associate for a couple of years (as I was promoted to trainer), I wasn't qualified for the open management

position. However, neither of them had any floor experience for the teams in which they were leading until I trained them.

5. This is why a large company should not hire in spouses and place them in management positions within the same department.

Over the previous six months leading up to this, I had dealt with a bunch of issues. First, I was moved over to another department to 'safeguard' me from retaliation for actually doing my job, which was reporting consistently poor preforming associates. (Another issue with senior management hiring in family and friends.) Then I was given double the responsibilities without an increase in pay or title adjustment. After that, for the first time in seven years I was not awarded a cost of living raise or a bonus. Now, this?! So, yes. I got pissed the hell off!

So, what did I do next? Well, like a good (and smart) girl, I saved the call, sent it to myself, and automatically contacted Human Resources. The next day I received a meeting request to discuss the recorded call with one of the Human Resource Business Partners from another one of our other office locations. During that conversation, the Human Resource Business Partner seemed to be more focused on why I listened to the call, than the content of the call. She attempted to ask me the same question multiple times, only to receive the same response. Nice try, lady. I may be ten kinds of crazy, but I am no damn dummy. However, I seen EXACTLY where this was going.

That Friday, at noon to be exact, I was pulled into the Human Resource Business Partners' office from my physical location, where two members of the Human Resource department were sitting. I was then informed that I was being placed on "Administrative Leave", which was suspension with pay, while they "investigate concerns" they had with MY conduct regarding this issue. Okay. Interesting, but okay.

The following Monday afternoon, I received a call from two of the Human Resource Business Partners; the one from my physical location and the one I had spoken with over the phone one week prior. I was informed that they did some research and had reports that I was listening to hundreds of calls I wasn't supposed to be listening to. The truth is, I could have very well listened to the amount of calls they had claimed I had. I honestly have no clue. However, according to the official (on company letter head and signed) copy of my job responsibilities I was provided in 2013, as well as the shady-ass non-official (that was NOT on company letter head and NOT signed by myself and management) list they provided me a few months ago, this *was* part of my job description. If it wasn't, why was I given access to it? I mean, wouldn't *that* violate the "Acceptable Use Policy" under management procedures which states they are to provide employees *only* access to programs/materials they are supposed to have to perform their assigned tasks... especially since access to program content can be filtered out by management who has to approve specified access? Oh yeah, I almost forgot. The policies in the handbook are subjective. None the less, I digress.

The Human Resource Business Partners ended the call by stating they would need to take a few more days to 'investigate things further'. Which, let's be honest, meant they want a few more days to build a case as to why they are going to let me go. I mean, now I'm more of a liability than an asset. I've been there too long and clearly know too much. However, with as much time and energy I have put into the company... and *literal* blood, sweat, and tears I have shed on behalf of it... I was not going to allow them that opportunity. I was done. Done with fighting for my right to do my job. Done with allowing them to push me around and not admit their truths or wrong-doings. Done with having daily anxiety attacks about what kind of retaliation or harassment I was going to be subjected to that day. Just, done.

That evening, I wrote and submitted my resignation letter. I explained how grateful I was for the experience I was able to obtain as being a member of the company, how I wished nothing less than the best for all of the associates, and that I thought it was in the best interest of both the company's time and resources, as well as my time and health, to "sever ties effective immediately".

Yes, I know. Some of you may think that I allowed them to win. Yes, I did. However, though they may have won the battle… they definitely didn't win the war. Sure, I lost a steady paycheck temporarily, but there isn't a price you can put on peace-of-mind. In the end, they lost much more.

They lost a tenured employee who had invested genuine energy, time, and heart into not only the company, but also each associate's development. They lost a member of their work family who risked almost everything to try to protect their credibility. I guess no-one ever taught them that you should never try to bite the hand that is trying to keep you fed.

Almost two weeks after I submitted my letter of resignation, I received an official "Cease and Desist" letter from the company. This letter, which was mailed to me via express mail and required my signature, stated that they were demanding that I discard of any protected health information and non-public company-based-process resources I may have immediately and if I didn't, I would be facing legal actions. Whiskey-Tango-Foxtrot?! I have NONE of those things, and they *know* that, which is why all of that seemed very 'extra' and ridiculous to me. However, what I actually DO have (and the ONLY things I have), are the copies of all the email communications that occurred between myself, two of my supervisors, three Directors, Human Resources (including the Director of HR), the Chief of Compliance, the Chief Officer of my department, and the Legal Counsel from over the last year of my employment which include the concerns I brought to their attention about the actions occurring within the department I initially worked for, the treatment I was receiving, as well as the request for updates to my employment record which were never corrected and/or adjusted. I also kept a copy of the useless Associate Handbook, as well as both official and unofficial copies of my job responsibilities. If I put my name on it, had to sign for it, or it affected my livelihood... I printed and kept it.

Before I close out this book, and all these chapters in my life permanently, I wanted to share a few words with any executives who run and/or manage big time corporations. Please make note of the following points because the morale and professional progression of your company may one day depend on these factors. Also, I'm taking this opportunity to speak on behalf of some of the associates that did not (or do not) have the courage to speak up on their own. I made them some promises, I now intend to keep!

1. Do not treat your associates who are in entry level positions like they are bottom-feeders. The truth is that they are usually the foundation of your company and without them the rest of your departments would not be able to function properly.

2. Do not place people in management roles who do not or have not actually preformed the tasks their associates are preforming. Hiring someone from the outside and placing them in a management role, only to have their assigned senior associates show them how to perform the tasks they perform on a daily basis, and then tasking the newly hired managers to monitor and address the associates' productivity does nothing but discourage your tenured employees. It promotes resentment and discourages those who have *already* invested time enough to train your newly hired managers from wanting to progress within your company.

3. Drug test and do background checks on your employees regularly. Do you really want someone coming to work high as a kite on a daily basis speaking on behalf of your clients and writing half-ass information in your databases? Do you honestly want someone who has committed a crime *after* you hired them to be someone running a department and managing some of your projects? Do you want people like that representing your company? I didn't think so. Do the checks. Do them *regularly*.

4. Stop treating your adult employees like children. If

your managers feel the need to micromanage their employees, maybe it is time to re-evaluate your hiring managers and why they are having difficulties selecting competent employees. Maybe if your hiring managers focused more on the quality of the candidates they are recruiting than they do hiring in friends and family, or family *of* friends, your management teams could focus more on their responsibilities versus making sure everyone else was doing theirs efficiently and to your standards.

5. Stop creating a hostile work environment. By allowing those who fall short on their quality and task completion deadlines the same opportunity to 'interview' for promotable positions as those who consistently meet/exceed quality and productivity standards, you are giving the impression that being a hand-working, efficient, and dedicated employee has no relevance or bearings. To hell with "Equal Opportunity"! If they want it, make them earn it, and then offer (yes, I said OFFER) promotable positions to those who have proven to be reliable. After all, what is the point of doing quality assessments, having associates write/complete goals, and having employee personnel files if they are not going to have a purpose?

6. If an associate escalates concerns for the company all the way up to your Legal department, and willingly chooses *not* to hide behind anonymity to do so, *listen* to them and take it *seriously*. Someone would not risk being a bigger target of harassment, bullying, and mistreatment unless they believed that what they were trying to fight for would (in the end) possibly save jobs and the company's credibility. Punish them less and appreciate them more.

I put seven years into the company. And, as much as I would love to say that I give zero damns about it, I think we all know that would be a complete lie. I guess the truth is that if I didn't genuinely care about the company, or each of the associates, I wouldn't be so damn pissed off.

To answer some possible lingering questions: No, I don't think the C.E.O. and founder of the company knows what all is *really* going on within his company. At least, I would like to believe he doesn't. This company is his baby. Yes, the husband and wife are *still* working for the company in management positions within the same department and location which means plotting against people's (who are not their personal friends) succession will continue. And, no... I wouldn't trade the seven years I fought on the behalf of the company or its associates for anything, even if those I worked closest with (some of which even broke bread with my family and were guests at my wedding) have all have been advised that it was in their best interest to not speak with me by senior management. I know, real mature.

Lastly, I would like all of the associates and agents I trained, mentored, and coached over the past several years to know that I *have always* and *will always* believe in your potential. Please remember what I told you all during your new hire training classes and coaching sessions. Focus on *your* development. Do not feed into any of the clique behaviors. Come to work, do your job, focus on your career, and then go the hell home. Maintain your integrity and remember that just because everyone is doing it, doesn't make it right... and it is *always* better to stand out than it is to blend in.

After everything I have been subjected to and had to endure, I have come to the conclusion that some people are simply not cut out to play on the corporate-politics playground... especially me. I guess it may be true that I am just too much of a blue-collar girl to play in the sandbox of this kind of white-collar world.

ABOUT THE AUTHOR

B. LOUISE LOCASTRO

B. Louise LoCastro graduated high school in 1999, and proceeded to graduate from college in 2001, with a Psychology Degree specializing in Human Services. She is currently residing in the same city in which she was born and raised in. She has an open mind and a sharp tongue, with a passion for truth. Her writings are brutally honest, and decorated in humor.

Welcome to the writings of a woman ready to take on the world!